No Drama First-Time Mama

No Drama First-Time Mama

A Practical Guide to Living Your
Best Life as a New Mother

EMILY LAMMERS

At the risk of sounding trite, I would like to dedicate this book to all the moms and moms-to-be out there. We're all in this experience together, because there's truly nothing like it. A special thank you to my friends who took the plunge into motherhood and shared their valuable wisdom and support with me (some of which is included in this book), and to my very own mom who has always been the type of mom I aspire to be.

Contents

OMG, I'm Going To Be A Mom

"Having a baby is like getting a tattoo on your face. You really need to be certain it's what you want before you commit."

~ Elizabeth Gilbert, author of *Eat, Pray, Love*

I put off having a baby for a long time. I knew it was something I eventually wanted to do, but truth be told, it just didn't sound fun. I liked the idea of a snuggly little baby and an intoxicating new kind of love, but those positives were overshadowed by the horror stories I had heard regarding sleep deprivation, constant stress, deteriorating relationships, and generally turning into a tiny human's personal slave. In my mind, becoming a mother meant saying goodbye to life as I knew it. And as someone who loves to have options, while at the same time being a bit indecisive, the most terrifying aspect of having a child was the permanence of it all. There was literally no out if I ended up disliking the whole thing.

On top of those preconceived notions and fears were the ridiculous expectations that society has cruelly dumped on new moms. Gone are the days when one could confidently choose to formula feed or rub whiskey on a baby's gums for teething pain. Moms these days face intense pressure to breastfeed, use all organic and natural products, stimulate their child with developmentally appropriate activities, lose the baby weight in weeks, maintain a spotless mid-century modern home, go back to killing it at their job, and spend every free moment doting on their little nugget. Oh! And this picture-perfect mom life must obviously be displayed for all to see via an expertly curated social media feed. I exaggerate slightly (you can have a spotless modern farmhouse home), but the pressure to be a super mom is omnipresent given the rampant virtue and status signaling in today's culture.

Despite all of this, I eventually conceded that I wasn't getting any younger and decided it was time to embark on Project Baby. Once pregnant with my son, I spent a lot of time thinking about what I wanted my life as a new mom to be like. I wanted to continue doing the things I loved — traveling, being active, writing, hanging out with friends, and the like. I also wanted to continue growing a career that I had invested a lot of time and energy in, while reluctantly acknowledging that some sacrifices would likely need to be made. Most of all, I still wanted to feel like myself even if my life had fundamentally and irreversibly changed. I was also very clear that I did not want to turn into a "mom martyr" who sacrifices her entire life in order to do anything and everything for her kids, and acts holier-than-thou about it to boot.

My husband thankfully had a similar vision of our soon-to-be family unit. We talked extensively about not wanting our son to completely change our dynamic, and we felt very strongly that he should have to fit into our lives, as opposed to us rearranging our lives around him. He would need to go along with our decisions and do whatever we wanted to do since, by gosh, we were the adults. Now, I can almost hear some seasoned parents snickering behind my back and I'll admit that some of these goals were aspirational. *Of course* we realized that having a baby was going to have a big impact on our everyday existence. However, we were hopeful that the change wouldn't need to be as drastic and jarring as we had been led to believe.

It is unsurprising then, that I ended up taking a very mom-centric approach to motherhood. Some might consider it a bit selfish, but personally I think it's just savvy. My view is that as a mom, it is both reasonable and advisable to prioritize yourself in order to counterbalance the extreme focus on the baby. Take a look at the resources and literature out there for new moms — the vast majority of it concerns the baby. Babies generally get around six check-ups during their first year, while moms typically get one. People will always ask how a new baby is doing, but how many of those same people ask about the mom? Say what you will about former British Royal Meghan Markle, but her emotional admission that "not many people have asked if I'm okay" following the birth of her son was an important moment for all of us mums (see what I did there?) There are certainly good reasons to be focused on the baby — they are rather helpless, after all — but a mother's well-being does not necessarily need to come at the expense of her baby's.

I'm an advocate for new moms being deliberately self-centered because I truly feel that self-care is the foundation for success and happiness as a parent. Turns out the old oxygen mask directive of helping yourself before you help others is applicable far beyond the airplane. If you are struggling and decidedly not in a good place, those around you are sure to be negatively affected. On the flip side, if you are healthy, happy, and fulfilled, you'll be in a position to be the best possible mother to your baby. I would also note that being selfish is relative when it comes to being a mom. Regardless of your unique circumstances, you'll inevitably be doing a boatload for your child each and every day. There is no reason to feel that you are not doing enough — you are literally keeping someone alive — and as an extension there should be absolutely no shame in caring for yourself alongside of caring for your baby.

I'm confident that employing this mindset set me up for success as a first-time mom. As a long-time baby skeptic, I am honestly still shocked by how much I enjoyed my son's baby phase, as are many of my friends. My aim is to share some of the philosophies, strategies, and tactics that helped me survive, and dare I say thrive, in the first year with my baby. Whether you're a mom-to-be or already in the thick of it (because let's be honest, there is no ramping up period), I hope you'll find my learnings and overall approach to motherhood helpful in navigating your own journey.

I do feel it's important to note that my message is not "do as I did and everything will be a piece of cake." Any way you slice it, being a new mom is HARD. Additionally, kids can be dramatically different from one another and some are just more challenging than others. (May the odds be ever in your favor!) By the same token, your particular circumstances will invariably affect your experience. I was lucky to have good health, financial security, a generous maternity leave, and many friends who were already moms. However, I didn't have any family nearby and I was flying solo every weekday morning because of my husband's work schedule. Everyone will have their own pros and cons, so I recommend focusing on what you can actually control — ahem, your attitude and actions — instead of dwelling on difficulties specific to your child or lifestyle.

Now for one last bit of housekeeping. There are many personal anecdotes in the following chapters and since my son is not old enough to provide consent to be mentioned by name, I've decided to compromise by using his nickname — Schnitzel. What can I say? He has an über German name and I also happen to find him delicious.

Alright, my friends. The backdrop is set. Let's dive into how to live your best life as a first-time mama. It's going to be fun, trust me.

Birth Plans Are Overrated

"There's a whole birthing plan, but what is the plan other than to get it out? I mean, there isn't an option to kind of keep it in, is there?"

~ **Keira Knightley, actress**

As far as I can tell, birth plans are a relatively recent phenomenon. I believe my mom's birth plan, along with much of her cohort's, went something along the lines of: go to hospital, have baby. I mean, the big excitement in the 1980's was epidurals going mainstream. Woo wee! (But in all seriousness, thank heavens for that). Suffice it to say, things have changed quite a bit over the last thirty-some years. There have been continued medical advancements, a trend towards "natural" (i.e. unmedicated) births, and perhaps more than anything, a movement towards the mother playing a much bigger role in determining how the birth should, in theory, happen. Enter, the birth plan.

Despite the title of this chapter, I think there are undoubtedly some positive things to come from the rise of birth plans. Namely, there is now more of a dialogue between moms and their healthcare providers, likely resulting in better preparation for said moms and potentially better outcomes all the way around. About a month before my due date, I was presented with a four-page Birth Day Preferences form that invited me to comment on a number of situations that I might expect to encounter and note any particular wishes. While I ended up writing very little on the forms -- guess I was going with the lazy mom's birth plan — I appreciated having the opportunity to think through various scenarios and chew on whether I felt super strongly about any aspects of the birth.

My big beef with birth plans is that they can create the illusion that a birth can be orchestrated in a very specific way. This can lead to serious disappointment if and when things don't go according to plan. In fact, the "plan" in the term birth plan is a bit of a misnomer given how truly unpredictable giving birth can be. Sure, it's easy to control whether icicle lights adorn your delivery room or whether Enya plays in the background, but when it comes to the big stuff such as how the baby is actually delivered, all bets are off.

I know several moms who had their hearts set on a specific type of birth, be it vaginal, unmedicated, home birth, or otherwise, only to have their dreams crushed when they needed an emergency C-section. For some, not having the delivery go exactly as envisioned can be tough pill to swallow on top of what is already a crazy emotional process. While your major preferences should certainly be communicated to your delivery team in advance, my advice is to stay flexible and expect the unexpected. If you are able to stay focused on the big picture (ie. the health and safety of your baby) instead of the details, you'll likely have a much better chance of being at peace no matter how things go down.

The same mindset applies to expectations for the immediate aftermath of delivery. Giving birth is intense, both physically and mentally. And while popular culture would lead us to believe there will be a picture-perfect moment when your beautiful baby is placed in your arms and you have an instantaneous connection and an overwhelming sense of joy, this isn't always the case. It certainly wasn't for me. In fact, I shrieked when they plopped Schnitzel onto my chest and felt more bewildered than anything else. Some moms won't even have the potential for such an awkward postpartum encounter if either party requires additional medical attention. This is undoubtedly disappointing, and several moms I know who have been in this situation described feeling robbed. But this just underscores my point that many "meet your baby" experiences are more complex and involve much a broader range of emotions than you might expect.

There is also the chance that you may not have the happy homecoming experience you had envisioned. Hardly anyone plans for their unborn child to have an extended stay in the neonatal intensive care unit (NICU), but it can and does happen, particularly in the case of premature babies. Several good friends of mine had preemies who were in the NICU for several weeks, and while I cannot even pretend to comprehend what that experience must be like, I can relay the advice they would give to other moms in this boat. Namely, allow yourself to feel upset, empty, detached, confused, and all the other feelings, trust the doctors and nurses, celebrate the milestones, and cut yourself some slack (whether that means taking a day off from visiting the NICU, giving up on pumping breastmilk alone at all hours of the day, or acknowledging that it's ok not to feel happy). Most of all, try to remember that the vast majority of NICU babies eventually come home happy and healthy.

With all of that said, what meaningful things can you actually control? Knowledge and readiness, for one. In my opinion, a little preparation can go a long way in helping manage general expectations and fears around giving birth. I, like the vast majority of other soon-to-be-moms I have encountered, was somewhere between pretty nervous and downright terrified in the weeks leading up to the big event. A birth class, while certainly not necessary, can be helpful. Chances are you will forget at least 70% of the content, but at least you will have a better general idea of what to expect. Without my birth class, I would not have understood the different phases of labor and delivery, or filed away the random tip that aiming a blowdryer on your newborn's bare bum after a diaper change can really chill him out (seriously, try this one!) I also recommend doing a hospital tour so that you have a certain level of comfort with the environment and more importantly, you'll know exactly where to go and where to park when the action begins.

I gained additional comfort by talking to mom friends who I knew wouldn't sugarcoat things but who also wouldn't completely freak me out by divulging too many gory details. And as I thought through aspects of giving birth that I didn't really understand, I didn't hesitate to ask these friends or my OBGYN. Here's a quick smattering: *Would my water break?* Not necessarily. *What the hell is a mucus plug and would I notice when it falls out?* A jellyfish-like blob that blocks the cervix until the baby is ready to come out and once again, not necessarily. *How do you know when you're transitioning into active labor?* Everyone has their own special answer for that one, but thankfully a friend told me that some women throw up when it starts and therefore I wasn't overly anxious when I lost my lunch. *What if I never went into labor?* If you make it to around 41 weeks with nary a contraction, your medical team will likely try to induce labor with medication or other techniques. See? Not so scary, really.

If you're still hungry for information and don't have a good crew of people to consult, stick to that factual information on the internet and stay far, far away from any message boards. The Lucie's List blog (lucieslist.com) — a treasure trove of information, encouragement, and humor for new parents — has some solid straight talk on giving birth and postpartum topics. Whatever you do, try not to dwell on the unknowns or obsess over any specific scenarios as that will only heighten your anxiety.

There is so much anticipation that comes with the birth of your child, but to put it into perspective, it is only one very small part of the journey. As long as you and your baby are healthy, nothing else really matters that much. And if for some reason you are upset with how your birth experience turned out, take some time to acknowledge your feelings and share your frustration with your partner, parents, friends, or therapist. Then let it go. There are going to be so many more interesting and wonderful challenges that will demand your energy and attention.

Take It Easy
And Take All The Help You Can Get

"No one told me I would be coming home in diapers, too."

~ **Chrissy Teigen, model, tv personality, author**

T he early days at home with your baby are a weird and wonderful time. At least that's how I felt. My husband and I were surprisingly calm and mainly just super curious about our new little roommate. We had no idea what we were doing, but we improvised and managed to keep Schnitzel alive and mostly content. Sleep was limited, but we were energized by baby snuggles. With things generally going better than anticipated, I was eager to snap back to "normal life" and prove to myself and everyone else that this baby hadn't completely turned my world upside down.

Before 1 began knocking out items on my to-do list however, I remembered the advice a good friend and mom of two had given me a few weeks prior. We were taking a leisurely stroll, as super pregnant women do, and she warned me not to do *anything* for the first couple weeks after giving birth because overdoing it could really hinder my recovery. I don't remember her providing any supporting evidence —

strange, because she's a lawyer — but based on her conviction alone I took the message to heart. Truth be told, I also felt physically worse than I had expected (because seemingly no one wants to tell you the whole truth about their post-delivery state), so taking it easy seemed like a good idea.

Then at some point during this immediate postpartum period I stumbled upon a viral mommy post of a Dixie paper plate with a measuring tape showing its 8½ inch diameter. The shock value was in learning that the plate is the same diameter of an average placenta. So after you've given birth and delivered your placenta, another fun little bonus that no one talks about, you're left with a wound the size of a flipping dinner plate on the inside of your uterus from where that bizarro organ used to be attached. This horrifying discovery reaffirmed my intent to continue to do as little as humanly possible while my body healed itself.

A big part of my recovery strategy was to simply say yes to anything and everything that was offered to me. My parents wanted to fly out after my husband went back to work and do all the cooking, cleaning, and grocery shopping (and okay, some baby holding) for two weeks. Umm, yes please. Generous friends asked if it would be alright to stop by with dinner or have some sent over. You betcha — which day? Even my husband, who is a helpful and conscientious human, offered to do more housework, errands, and infant care than I would've expected, and I gladly took him up on all of his offers. If there ever was a time to be lazy, this was it.

I tried to limit my workload to feeding, changing, and holding the baby, and I practiced diligent postpartum self-care (hello, sitz baths[1]

---

[1] A warm, shallow bath for soaking your undercarriage. You can ask for a sitz bath basin (it's kind of like a mobile bidet) in the recovery room or order one online along with some soothing sitz bath salts. And while we're on the

and padsicles[2]!). I took naps or at least lay down whenever an opportunity presented itself. And when it came to physical activity, I barely left my apartment during the first two weeks. The sedentary life made me a little crazy because I thrive on both physical activity and getting shit done. But every time I started feeling antsy, I thought of the plate-sized wound I ostensibly still had and reminded myself that my recovery was more important.

I feel that my efforts paid off since I came out of the first month feeling mostly intact from both a mental and physical standpoint. This was in spite of my almost "advanced maternal age" of 34¾. I wasn't in any position to fully resume my active pre-baby life, but I also wasn't a decrepit zombie. All things considered, it felt like a win.

So, what if you don't have an army of family and friends at your beck and call, or are particularly concerned about your ability to cope with a newborn and adequately recover? For starters, you may want to consider a night nurse. For a pretty penny, these fairy godmother types will come to your home in the evenings to assist with feeding and handle the changing and soothing, thereby allowing you and your partner to get at least a few hours of shuteye here and there. Another option is a postpartum doula, who will usually do all of this and more at any hour of the day. Postpartum doulas also typically have a focus on the health and well-being of the mother and may provide mentorship regarding the adjustment to being a parent.

Most moms I know have sourced these helpers through friends, online mom groups, their hospital, or DONA International (dona.org) and hired them ahead of the baby's arrival, however I've also known some to call in help after the fact. If you're interested but

---

topic, do yourself a favor and order an angled peri bottle because the lame ones they give you at the hospital don't even begin to do the job.

2 Maxi pads doused with witch hazel, aloe, and perhaps some essential oils, that are then rewrapped and put in the freezer. Make them ahead of time. Lots of them.

not quite ready to commit, it might behoove you to start speaking with some to get a sense for their personalities and availability should you find yourself needing reinforcement down the road.

In my somewhat judgy pre-baby days, I thought that night nurses and postpartum doulas were a ridiculous luxury and that first-time moms who arranged outside help months in advance of their due date were essentially admitting they couldn't hack it on their own. I've since changed my tune. While I did not end up hiring either, I am all for putting yourself in the best position to stay afloat during the first several weeks. I've had many a mom friend who has found this sort of professional help to be an absolute lifesaver. One had a night nurse from the onset but found herself "ready to snap" after a month because her son would hardly sleep during the day and wouldn't tolerate the stroller or carrier. She promptly went out an hired a doula to come three days a week and was able to function like a real human again. And you can bet that I would've scrambled to line up someone if Schnitzel had colic or if I felt myself slipping down a deep dark hole of sleep deprivation or depression. If your budget allows for some regular extra help that you know you would like or perhaps already really need, I say knock yourself out.

One last word on hired help — if you're a mom of multiples (twins or more, for those not down with the lingo), by all means, get yourself some. Now. First of all, you're going to want an extra set of hands on an extremely regular basis. Secondly, it might be helpful if those hands aren't related to you. One of my friends was lucky enough to be living in the same neighborhood as her parents when her twins were born and as thankful as she was for their near daily help, she wouldn't recommend relying exclusively on family members. "I just didn't feel like I could boss around my mom since I wasn't paying her," she said. Noted.

To further minimize your workload, I also recommend outsourcing all the mundane tasks you possibly can. While perhaps less demanding than infant care, pesky tasks such as cooking, cleaning, and shopping still take considerable time and energy, both of which are at a premium as a new mom. Get a housecleaner. Have groceries delivered. Order takeout often. Use a laundry service if you feel so inclined. Buy anything and everything you need from Amazon and set up Subscribe and Save[3] for your recurring purchases. Yes, it's annoying to pay extra for things you used to do for yourself, but the circumstances will have changed dramatically and quite frankly, these tasks aren't worth your time anymore. Go ahead, treat yourself to the luxury of convenience.

The concept of making sure you have all the help you need may be just as important later on as you settle into your new reality of mom life and the initial excitement from your "village" begins to wane. Sleep deficits and stress can build up, going back to work can throw a wrench in your routine, your baby could have a dreaded sleep regression, and so on. I remember seeing a former classmate post on Facebook saying that she was really struggling with caring for her six-month-old and soliciting friends to sign up for a meal train. I was struck by the courage it took to admit she needed help, as well as her initiative to do something about it. Bravo, fellow mama!

I've also noticed posts in my social media communities from moms who feel like they are drowning and are seeking support or advice. Nearly every such post is followed by a cascade of encouraging messages, kind offers, and helpful suggestions. Should you find yourself struggling, don't be afraid to throw up an SOS and seek out whatever kind of support you need, be it hiring outside help, calling

---

[3] I didn't know what this was until I had a baby. For anyone else in the dark, it's exactly what it sounds like. You can pick from thousands of discounted household items and automatically have them delivered every month with the option to skip or cancel at any time. The real kicker -- 20% off diapers!

on family and friends, or simply getting emotional support. It could mean the difference between just a rough patch and a very serious situation[4].

As women, we so often put our heads down and soldier on regardless of the circumstances. This can be especially true with the transition to motherhood. I certainly felt a heightened sense of responsibility to my family and a strong desire to keep all the balls in the air and be everything to everyone. But thankfully I realized early on that there was no need to play the hero by trying to do it all on my own. Asking for help and outsourcing isn't admitting defeat — it's just being smart.

---

[4] Mental health is obviously of the utmost importance when it comes to having a baby, and as such, it is addressed separately in a subsequent chapter.

Fed Is Best

"It's okay not to breastfeed, or only be able to do it for a short time. There, I said it."

~ Sarah Schmidt, an ordinary mom who had the courage to put that on the internet for all the world to see

I was pretty anxious about a lot of things when it came to having a baby, but perhaps none more so than breastfeeding. Women these days are beaten over the head with the belief that "breast is best" from the moment of conception, if not before. Expectant mothers are meant to feel that it is the only acceptable choice, and to not partake would be doing their children a major disservice. No pressure.

I had heard that breastfeeding wasn't always as easy as one might expect for something so fundamental to the perpetuation of humankind, so naturally I bought a 337-page book dedicated to the topic to allay my fears. I didn't even make it halfway through before I became entirely overwhelmed. My only major takeaway? I absolutely, positively should be breastfeeding and if I got to a point where I didn't think I was able to, I probably wasn't trying hard enough. I chucked the book and tried to forget about it all for the rest of my pregnancy.

Then Schnitzel arrived. It was go time. Except it didn't really go at all. I was confused that there was no milk. *Did no one have the decency to tell me this or had I just quit the book too soon?!* I was shocked to learn in the recovery room that milk doesn't come in until 2-5 days after the birth (and often towards the end of that range for mothers who have a C-section). I was matter-of-factly told that I was supposed to keep my baby alive for the first few days with a tiny bit of pre-milk golden goo call colostrum. Besides being totally weirded out that my body was basically producing honey, I also had no idea if Schnitzel was getting anything to eat via my clumsy initial attempts to breastfeed. His hapless chomping also really hurt.

A severe, Eastern Bloc nurse who was making the rounds on my second day in recovery essentially told me that the whole nursing thing probably wasn't going to work out for me. Then she took what can only be described as an Ace bandage tube top, cut two small holes a la Regina George in *Mean Girls*, and hooked me up to a medical grade pump. My husband and I were then instructed to use tiny syringes to capture the small bit of colostrum that clung to the sides of the flanges and squirt it into Schnitzel's mouth. It was stressful and many severely hormonal tears were shed, but least the word "flanges" never failed to make me laugh.

By the time we were discharged from the hospital, Schnitzel had lost more that 10% of his birthweight, which is the threshold for concern though not entirely abnormal. The doctors spoke to us about the need to potentially supplement with formula. *But how could I live with myself? I might have been a formula baby but my Schnitzel sure as hell couldn't be one!*

We went to the pediatrician's office the following day for a weight check, and while the seventy-five-year-old male doctor on duty was unable to weigh in on my breastfeeding form, he did confirm that

Schnitzel wasn't in dire condition. He also arranged for a lactation consultant to visit my apartment later in the day. While I was relieved to have help on the way, I also felt disappointed that I had seemingly failed to adequately provide for my child when he'd only been alive for a mere seventy-two hours. Thankfully the lactation consultant told me that everyone has problems (mostly true), gave me some pointers, prepped me for the entire breastfeeding journey, and basically held my hand and told me everything was going to be okay. It was money well spent.

Over the next several days Schnitzel and I found our groove, although truth be told, neither one of us was ever really psyched about breastfeeding. Besides being physically uncomfortable, I found serving as Schnitzel's sole source of sustenance to be mentally exhausting. I never once felt the intoxicating letdown sensation that breastfeeding enthusiasts rave about. And to top things off, Schnitzel was what the experts call a "disorganized feeder" who lacked focus and rhythm. Our feeds in the early months were close to hour-long marathons where seemingly nothing was achieved besides me catching up on *Bachelor in Paradise*. Even when he eventually got his act together, there was no magical bond between the two of us whilst nursing.

But before I get too negative, let me be crystal clear that if you turn out to be one of those lucky moms for whom breastfeeding comes easily, or if you really truly love it once you get the hang of it, that is fantastic! By all means, I'm glad that someone enjoys the experience. My message is aimed at the other faction of moms who find breastfeeding difficult, unpleasant, stressful, and in the worst cases, downright soul-crushing.

If breastfeeding turns out not to be your friend for any number of reasons, I would encourage you to attempt an objective assessment of your situation. First of all, are you continuing to stick with it because you steadfastly believe it is a must from a health perspective, or more so because it's so strongly perceived as the right thing to do? Secondly, how big of a toll is breastfeeding taking on you and your baby? Sore nipples are one thing, but if your baby isn't getting enough to eat, thereby forcing you to nurse at all hours of day and night, thereby making you both exhausted and irritable, that is quite another. If breastfeeding is having a meaningfully negative impact on your overall mental well-being and your ability to cope with the challenges of being a new mom, it might be time to revise your breastfeeding strategy. Options include exclusive pumping (notoriously difficult to sustain for long periods of time), supplementing with formula, or switching to formula altogether.

Now, it would be naïve of me to suggest that the decision to alter your breastfeeding plans is easy and painless. Like nearly everything when it comes to your child, breastfeeding is an incredibly personal decision, and those wacky hormones can make it even more difficult to be rational. I have heard many moms who have had difficulty with breastfeeding, first-timers and veterans alike, confess that they would feel like failures for modifying their approach or giving it up completely. I get it. Our nanny blew through my paltry stash of frozen breastmilk in my very first week back at work and I beat myself up over my body not being able to hack six months of exclusive breastfeeding. But the reality was that Schnitzel needed more to eat and it was no time for me to be unreasonable or self-loathing. Once I started supplementing with formula I got over things fairly quickly, and immensely enjoyed the new-found freedom of not being his only food option.

Similarly, I've witnessed several mom friends begrudgingly adjust their breastfeeding plans after prolonged struggles and their relief has been palpable. One of my friends was never able to nurse because she initially couldn't express milk and, in her words, her son "balled up his hands in fists and beat my breasts while screeching like a baby pterodactyl." When her milk fully came in she decided to pump exclusively, and kept it up for several weeks despite growing increasingly frustrated and exhausted. She was close to her breaking point at her postpartum checkup, but the OBGYN recommended that she not stop pumping as breastmilk was clearly best for the baby. Then said OBGYN had the audacity to mention that her son could still get into Harvard even if she did switch to formula (which was doubly insulting since said friend went to Princeton). Thankfully this friend refused to feel shamed by the OBGYN — or by the pediatric nurse at her son's practice who encouraged her to just keep up the pumping until the end of flu season (only another six months!) — and decided that what was best for her was best for her baby. She began to supplement with formula and immediately had a new lease on life.

Of course, not all medical professionals will be this judgmental. Another friend who experienced "serious trauma" in trying to breastfeed her first child, including a staph infection in her nipple (CAN YOU EVEN?!), threw in the towel at the suggestion of her pediatrician. She said it was as if the clouds had parted when she was no longer fighting the mental, physical, and logistical fight that breastfeeding can entail.

Should you find yourself in a pit of despair when it comes to breastfeeding, please don't let societal pressure get the best of you. Your sanity is a much more important factor in your ability to provide for your baby than the source of his milk. Let's all please agree that fed (and sane) is best.

I've spent a lot of time talking about boobs, but I'd like to add a note on bottles while we're on the topic of feeding. One of the most important things I learned from my short time with my lactation consultant was when to introduce the bottle. She was quick to tell me about the magic window between three to four weeks when a newborn is still malleable enough to easily learn how to feed from two different sources. This comes up real quick when you are not yet sleeping more than a few hours at a time, so try not miss it. I easily got Schnitzel going on the bottle at the beginning of the window and not only did the little turkey seemed to prefer it, but it seemed to help him gain weight and sleep for longer stretches. More importantly, "the freedom bottle," as another friend of mine calls it, gave me the flexibility to go to bed before the last feeding of the day or go out by myself for a few hours at a time. Freedom indeed!

But what if you've already missed the magic window? My unscientific advice would be to immediately jam a bottle into your baby's gummy little mouth and stick with it until you get some uptake. The ultimate goal here is to make sure your baby will take a bottle before you absolutely need her to. I've heard stories about so-called bottle interventions with older babies, and it sounds like the last thing a nervous new mom would want to worry about just before going back to work or leaving town for a couple of days.

Sleep Well, My Dear... In Your Own Room

"Babies smell sweeter when they are sleeping."

~ Anonymous

S leep has to be one of the toughest and touchiest subjects when it comes to life with a baby, and seemingly everyone has an opinion. I'm not going to weigh in on the sleep training debate, as it's well covered and I have nothing new to add. Instead I'd like to focus on something even more fundamental that you will be forced to reckon with as soon as you bring your baby home — rooming assignments. However, unlike sleepaway camp or freshman dorms, in this particular instance you actually get to call the shots. While potentially controversial, I've decided to share my approach as I feel it was very important to my success as a new mom and also helped set the tone for my entire relationship with Schnitzel.

I'll just come right out and say it — I am unapologetically against co-sleeping, be it standard issue room sharing or full-on bed sharing. The main reason for this is that sleep is oh-so-important for new moms and I believe that the farther apart from your baby you sleep, the better everyone's sleep has the potential to be. Besides a first-time mother's psyche to contend with (it is so much easier to check on the baby every five minutes if he is only two feet away), babies make some very strange and surprisingly loud noises in their sleep. Furthermore, I think it's both healthy and helpful to set some (very small) boundaries early on. I personally wanted to preserve my bedroom as my husband's and my own space, and have Schnitzel get used to his own digs as well.

Lest I come off as completely coldhearted, I'll concede that it can be more than a little nerve-racking to leave your impossibly small newborn all by his lonesome right away. Schnitzel's room was on a different floor on the other side of the apartment from our bedroom, which made for a bit of a pickle given my laser focus on my physical recovery (no stairs, thank you) and strict order to nurse every three hours until he got back to birthweight. As such, I decided to temporarily camp out in his room on the near lay-flat glider that I had strategically splurged on. I have more than a few friends who have taken it a step further and moved a couch into their baby's room — well played!

While my particular arrangement was not exactly cushy, it was workable in the short term and also allowed my husband to get some sleep, which was crucial as he'd had to go back to work after only a week of paternity leave. As soon as Schnitzel gained back his requisite poundage however, I moved back to my bedroom and never looked back. My trusty monitor provided all the reassurance I needed. I think it's fair to say that we both slept better in our own rooms, and I believe the nights apart early on taught him that he didn't need me all the time.

Now, I'm well aware that my strategy breaks with the American Academy of Pediatrics (AAP)'s recommendation to sleep in the same room as your baby on a different surface for the first six months, and ideally for the first year of life. This is purportedly to decrease the risk of sleep-related deaths such as Sudden Infant Death Syndrome

(SIDS). SIDS is incredibly tragic and downright terrifying to any new parent, but I still don't completely understand how sleeping in the same room as your baby is meaningfully preventative unless you happen to not actually be sleeping the entire time. Perhaps that's AAP's intent? Regardless, I decided to prioritize my quality of sleep over what I thought was likely a miniscule decrease in the risk of SIDS.

I felt vindicated for this decision when *Cribsheet: A Data-Driven Guide to Better, More Relaxed Parenting, From Birth to Pre-School* by Emily Oster was published shortly after Schnitzel's arrival. Oster, an economist and mother of two, notes that the four studies cited by the AAP show "small increases in SIDS rates for babies who sleep in their own room, but the results are not overwhelming." The aforementioned studies were quite small and incomplete — the use of a baby monitor was not considered, for example — and most weren't specifically designed to evaluate room sharing. I am decidedly not a medical expert or even an economist, but my takeaway was that we actually don't have convincing evidence on whether room sharing decreases SIDS or not. Oster herself concludes that the AAP's recommendation to room share through the baby's first year is overkill as the vast majority of SIDS deaths occur within the first four months. And she also cites a 2017 study that concluded that babies slept for longer stretches in their own room, presumably because it's quieter. Finally, she notes that most parents sleep better alone and that "parents being well rested in important too." Bingo.

I didn't bend my stance on sleeping arrangements much for special situations such as travel either. My husband and I would always try to book a suite if it was available and not outrageously expensive. Otherwise we'd drag the travel crib into the bathroom or hallway or closet — whichever option was furthest from our bed. We had absolutely no shame. Schnitzel once slept in a lovely rainforest shower at a resort in Napa, and I'd venture to say even liked it given his affinity for playing in empty showers as a toddler. Our philosophy was that it didn't make much sense to go on vacation if we definitely weren't going to sleep well.

Now that I've had the opportunity to swap sleeping stories with a myriad of other parents, I'm even more resolute in my beliefs, especially when it comes to bed sharing. It seems to me that many parents start out with a reasonable plan, be it baby in her own room or in her own sleeping compartment, but have trouble sticking to the plan when things get difficult. Many moms say it's just easier to have their baby in bed with them if they have to nurse or otherwise attend to her multiple times a night. And I don't doubt it! The problem is that it seems to be a slippery slope. If you bring your baby to bed once when you're exhausted, you're likely to feel comfortable with doing it again. And again. And again and again, until your little darling refuses to sleep anywhere else and no one in your house gets a good night's sleep for the next three years.

The short-term inconvenience just isn't worth the gamble of long-term pain, in my humble opinion. I certainly didn't relish crawling out of bed and climbing the stairs every time Schnitzel needed something in the middle of the night, but it was a tradeoff I was willing to make for the prospect of many solid nights of sleep down the road.

Sleeping turned out not to be a major issue for us[5], and while that is likely due to a number of factors including a hearty birth weight and

---

[5] I initially thought that having a baby meant I would not get a good night's sleep for the foreseeable future. Since seemingly every parent complains about sleeping, I figured most babies just didn't sleep. Not so! There are certainly many that aren't particularly good sleepers, but I was shocked to learn from a surprising number of friends that their babies were total champs. Apparently the poor sleepers just hog all the headlines. Try to keep this in mind before you pre-emptively sign yourself up for a sleep deprived life of misery. Stick to a routine, follow the 5 S's (swaddle, side or stomach position, shush, swing, suck), and stay optimistic. And if you are cursed with a crummy sleeper, take comfort in knowing that it will likely get better. And

mellow temperament, I really do believe that at least part of it was due to our separate sleeping quarters. It seemed that Schnitzel simply got comfortable with being alone in his crib and learning how to self-soothe from a very early age. And me? I went right back to logging several beautiful hours of uninterrupted sleep in the comfort of my own bed, with nothing but the dulcet tones of Schnitzel's sound machine coming through the monitor to keep me company.

As I've already admitted, there are no doubt many folks out there who wholeheartedly disagree with my logic and overall approach here. That's fine! There is no one right way to do this whole babyrearing thing. If you are a new mom who happens to be co-sleeping, either by choice or by accident, I do not judge. I would just encourage you to weigh your own sleeping needs and preferences alongside the other considerations when it comes to sleeping arrangements, both now and in the future.

---

maybe try sleep training when your baby is old enough (4-6 months) and don't let anyone make you feel bad about it. Oops, I weighted in after all.

Join A Mom Group

"As moms, we are in it together – raising the future. We are a tribe of future makers. So let's support each other."

~ Marissa Hermer, restauranteur, author, and reality tv star

T he mere thought of a mom group in my pre-baby days would've made me break out in hives. However, once I was in the final months of pregnancy and growing more anxious by the day, I was decidedly more open to the idea. A neighbor friend who had recently had a baby raved about the new mothers' group she had participated in and encouraged me to join the next cohort. It was a six-week "program" facilitated by a lovely French woman who was a lactation consultant and postpartum doula. I cringed at the enrollment fee — it was nearly as much as I had spent on my stroller — but eventually bit the bullet because I figured I needed all the coaching and support I could get.

I still remember the day of the first session vividly. Schnitzel was two and a half weeks old and it was our first solo outing together. I. Was. Nervous. I spent the better part of an hour getting ready, meticulously packing the diaper bag with everything I could possibly ever need, picking out respectable outfits for both of us, and debating whether the hilly ten-minute walk would be too strenuous for my recovering body. When I finally set out with the stroller, I was both exhilarated to be free from the confines of my apartment and terrified by what all could go wrong out in the open. We arrived late, as did almost all of the other moms and babies.

The next two hours were something straight out of a movie. Lots of boobs out, some spit up, babies wailing and being passed to the elegant French woman to be soothed, and more than a few tears. Schnitzel needed a diaper change at some point, a task which was to be executed in the same room as the gathering, and during the change he managed to pee straight up in the air and all over himself and me not once, but twice. Needless to say, we made a strong first impression. But as terrible and kumbaya as all this may sound, it was extremely therapeutic to share all of the complex emotions I had swirling around. Moreover, I left feeling like I had found people I could truly talk to. Sure, I had plenty of good friends who were also moms, but things with a baby change so quickly that there is something to be said for connecting with others who are in the throes of the exact same stage you are. A friend of mine who participated in a similar type of group in Washington DC reflected that it was almost better that the women in her group weren't her friends as there weren't any preconceived notions and everyone was starting from a clean slate in sharing their struggles and vulnerabilities.

Over the next several weeks we discussed all the practical things such as sleep tactics and training, breastfeeding and pumping strategies, behavioral and developmental milestones, childcare options, and going back to work logistics. Our facilitator always had useful insights to share with us, and the moms and I learned a lot from talking to each other too. We also discussed intensely personal topics ranging from dynamics with our spouses, feelings towards our parents and in-laws, sex (or lack thereof), and changes to our bodies. Cringeworthy perhaps, but man did it feel good to air things out in a supportive and judgement-free forum rather than letting it all fester. We also had an active WhatsApp group to ask for advice, share wins, and generally commiserate, which lived on well after the final official meeting.

Beyond the educational and emotional support my mom group provided, it also forced me to practice going out and about with Schnitzel very early on, albeit to a very safe space where meltdowns and diaper blowouts were celebrated. It is so easy to make excuses not to do things when you have a newborn, so getting into the habit of showing up every week regardless of how much sleep I had gotten or how disastrous my morning had been, helped me cultivate a can-do and will-do attitude right off the bat.

Based on this experience, I am obviously a proponent of the structured, part educational/part therapy type of mom group. However, I realize that this option may not exist everywhere or be logistically or financially feasible. Don't fret! There are plenty of other ways to share wisdom, laughs, and grievances with fellow moms. I've benefited from several less formal mom groups that I've been a part of, including city-specific Facebook groups (shout out to incredible Main Street Mamas community in San Francisco) and a Bay Area friends-of-friends group started by a college classmate. Still another community I benefited from was the moms and dads with whom I attended a baby care bootcamp class at my pediatrician's office. The facilitator, our practice's one-of-a-kind Nurse Judy, has witnessed such value created in these sessions that she has since become involved with launching Oath (oathcare.com), which dubs itself "onboarding for motherhood." A tailored parental cohort for sharing *and* medical support both mom and baby? Yes please!

To get a sense for what networks and offerings are available in your area, ask around, search online and on social media, or start striking up conversations with other new parents you happen to meet around your neighborhood. You will likely find many moms eager to connect.

And while I would stress the importance of having actual human contact through meet-ups to combat the isolation that can come with being a first-time mom, an email list or other digital forum can be an effective supplement.

Whatever you do, make the effort to connect with other moms in your area and general stage of motherhood, even if it feels awkward or putting yourself out there is the last thing you feel like doing. I have a few friends spread around the country who had their first children much earlier than the rest of us, and they have all recounted how lonely they felt during that time. They simply didn't have anyone nearby that could relate to what they were going through. Even the most well-meaning childless friend just won't get it. God knows I didn't.

Then, once you have a crew, be sure to ask questions and share experiences freely. You'll be amazed by the collective knowledge that exists. Polling your mom communities is also more efficient and typically way more constructive than going down the Google rabbit hole. In addition to learning from each other, you'll also likely be giving and receiving genuine support and encouragement. And unlike my structured newborn moms' program, no one can put a price on that.

Your Health Is Just As Important As Your Baby's

"Remember to take care of yourself. You can't pour from an empty cup."

~ Unknown

I've said it before and I'll say it again — your health and well-being are crucial to thriving as a new mom. Unfortunately, they are frequently overlooked given that most new moms are intensely focused on their baby's seemingly endless needs. It certainly doesn't help that the standard post-natal care in the US is woefully inadequate. Most moms can expect exactly one postpartum visit to their OBGYN, the six-week check-up, which typically consists of a physical exam, a short questionnaire designed to screen for postpartum mood disorders (PMADs), and a discussion regarding birth control. This check-up may or may not be comprehensive, and depending on where you are in your recovery, you may or may not know if you have any cause for concern. That's why I recommend doing self-check-ins throughout the entire first year to regularly assess how your mind and body are feeling during this time of major change.

Mental health is obviously the top priority given how prevalent PMADs are and how serious the effects can be. It's estimated that 15-20% of women will experience meaningful symptoms of depression or anxiety after the birth of a child. PMADs typically manifest between three weeks and three months after giving birth, however they can pop up at any point during the first year, hence the importance of routinely evaluating your mental state. For quick reference, I've listed some of the symptoms for the two most common PMADs and their largely overlapping risk factors below. I've starred the risk factors that have been the focus of previous chapters to underscore just how important these issues are, as well as point out that they are some of the only risk factors you can actually take steps to address.

Postpartum Depression Symptoms

- Feelings of anger or irritability

- Lack of interest in the baby

- Appetite and sleep disturbance

- Crying and sadness

- Feelings of guilt, shame, or hopelessness

- Loss of interest, joy, or pleasure in things you used to enjoy

- Possible thoughts of harming the baby or yourself

Postpartum Anxiety Symptoms

- Constant worry

- Feeling that something bad is going to happen

- Disturbances of sleep and appetite

- Inability to sit still

- Physical symptoms like dizziness, hot flashes, and nausea

Risk Factors

- Personal or family history with depression or anxiety

- Insufficient support in caring for your baby*

- Financial or marital stress

- Complications with conception, pregnancy, birth, or breastfeeding*

- Concurrent major life changes (loss, moving, job change)

- Giving birth to multiples

- Having a baby in the NICU

- Diabetes or thyroid imbalance

- Previous mood reaction to hormonal changes (PMS, premenstrual dysphoric disorder)

Source: postpartum.net

Despite not having any major risk factors, I was very nervous about PMADs as I had several friends who struggled with them. Thus, I was constantly monitoring my mood and stress level, and questioning whether I was developing a problem or just having a bad day. I also had conversations with my husband, parents, and a few close friends about my worries and asked them to kindly intervene if I started to seem not like myself.

You certainly don't need to be that obsessive, but I'd recommend doing an honest check in with yourself every now and then to assess whether you are consistently experiencing any PMAD symptoms. If you have any reason to think there may be a problem, talk to your OBGYN or primary care doctor stat. It's certainly nothing to be ashamed of — remember nearly *one in five* new moms will have some form of PMAD — and the sooner you address it via therapy, medication, or otherwise, the sooner you'll be on your way to more fully enjoying life with your baby.

A good friend of mine who had several of the above risk factors and ended up experiencing postpartum anxiety emphasized just how important a proactive approach is. She acknowledged that it was difficult to admit that there was a problem and deal with the stigma of being on "mommy pills," but waiting to get help only made things worse. "Even if you feel like you can make it through, kids can sense anxiety and depression. Getting on medication made me a calmer and better parent, and I just wish I would've done it sooner," she reflected.

While mental health is paramount, physical health is also important to keep tabs on given how hard growing, carrying, and birthing a baby can be on your body. As I discussed earlier, immediate postpartum recovery should be taken seriously, and even though our bodies are pretty miraculous at healing themselves, some issues tend to linger. Two of the most common physical ailments are diastasis recti, which is the separation of the abdominal muscles, and pelvic floor disorders, which can include incontinence and prolapse. In full disclosure, I was not familiar with any of those terms until I nervously started Googling whether all my parts would eventually go back to normal during a 3am feeding session. I will spare you the gory details — there is actually plenty of useful information on the internet and I've found @mypelvicfloormuscles on Instagram has some really helpful educational content — but the bottom line is that you don't have to live with these conditions, nor should you. There are specialists out there who can help, and treatment usually starts with simple exercises you can do at home. It's not fun stuff per se, but it's worthwhile. I speak from experience.

One final to-do on the personal health front is to re-establish your relationship with your primary care doctor within the first six months after giving birth. For better or for worse, I relied on my OBGYN for basically everything healthcare related for a nearly two-year span before, during, and after my pregnancy. At about nine months postpartum, I scheduled a checkup with my primary care doctor, mostly because it felt like something I should've done long ago. I was right. Turns out I was still on the "mini-pill" (progestin only, no estrogen) for birth control, which had some funky side effects and wasn't necessary since I was no longer breastfeeding. My doctor got that straightened out and provided some helpful tips on a couple other aspects of my postpartum health. Given the cliff in postpartum care after the six-week check-up, it's up to you to take ownership of your health and ensure that there is continuity in your postpartum care.

I fully realize that going to personal appointments when you are a new mom is easier said than done, but the truth is you'll likely never "have more time." It is essential for new moms prioritize their health and be aware of how their minds and bodies are feeling. What may initially seem like just a minor issue could chip away at your comfort or confidence, or spiral out of control if left untreated. If anything seems off, book that sitter and go get it checked out. The precious time you have with your baby is way too short to not be feeling your best.

Enable Independence

"You can't let the animals run the zoo."

**~ Kate from *Workin Moms*, the perfect show
to binge watch during this stage of life**

As an only child, I've always enjoyed my alone time and prided myself on being pretty self-sufficient. Needless to say, I had high hopes that my baby would not be the kid who needed to be held all the time, only to then turn into the toddler who constantly demanded my attention. Lofty? Perhaps. Unattainable? Unclear. As I nervously awaited Schnitzel's arrival, I vowed to do everything in my power to enable and cultivate his independence from the very beginning in the hopes that he might not annoy the living daylights out of me by age two.

However, it's difficult to know how you are actually going to react when your baby arrives and my early actions did not align with my goals. New moms are legitimately hard-wired to respond to their newborn babies. There is just something primal about the cry or coo of your own helpless child that tugs at your heartstrings and demands swift and immediate action. All a baby really needs in the first several weeks is to be fed, changed, and held, yet I felt compelled to try to

41

engage Schnitzel on a near constant basis. Never mind that I received hardly any positive reinforcement given his larval state. Thankfully our pediatrician sleuthed out my misguided efforts at his one-month check-up and gently told me that if he was blankly staring out the window during my stuffed animal musical performance, he just wanted to go the fuck to sleep. I suddenly realized that I would need to start fighting my natural instincts if I was going to keep the dream of an independent child alive.

I cooled my jets and got more comfortable with letting Schnitzel be the snoozy, disoriented marsupial that he was. But once he emerged from the newborn stage and become more interactive, I was confused and conflicted all over again. I wanted to be a great mom. Didn't that mean I should be playing with him all the time when he was alert? I polled my trusted veteran mom friends and quickly concluded that no, it did not. The moms of multiple children got an especially good laugh out of my inquiry.

Turns out young babies are plenty stimulated by just absorbing the world around them, and indeed Schnitzel liked playing in his activity gym, fondling toys, and looking around while out on walks seemingly as much as he enjoyed engaging with me. There is a balance to this, of course. I don't condone being on your phone for hours while your baby sits alone. But there's nothing wrong with regularly giving him the opportunity to entertain himself for a bit while you lightly supervise from afar. In addition to giving you a mental break or the opportunity to get some small tasks done, it helps set a precedent that you do not exist solely to serve or entertain your child.

As Schnitzel became older and more mobile, I further encouraged him to explore on his own. He could spend hours tearing apart the kitchen cabinets, rearranging the freezer drawer, or inspecting the washing machine, among other things. I'm sure the hardcore baby proofing crowd and the neatniks wouldn't approve of my free-range style, but as long as the sharp objects, choking hazards, and household cleaners have been cleared out and you're loosely keeping an eye on things, I don't see any reason why this shouldn't be a regular form of play. In fact, this was probably Schnitzel's preferred indoor activity for well over a year. He loved inspecting new objects and trying to figure out how things worked on his own with only an occasional explanation from his parents. I like to think that this helped cultivate his confidence as he understood we trusted him to explore without constant close supervision.

My laissez-faire approach also had the added benefit of making "no" a much more powerful directive. Based on my observations, a child is much more likely to respond to a stern "no" in regard to touching the oven if they haven't already heard it for thirty low-stakes infractions earlier in the day.

Despite my learning curve with how to handle awake time, my sleeping time game was strong right out of the gate. As discussed earlier, sleeping in separate rooms was a key piece of my strategy for enabling Schnitzel's independence. But beyond simple logistics, I didn't go running into his room to check on him the moment he made a peep. Whether it was in the middle of the night, first thing in the morning, or during naptime, I always waited a few minutes and watched the monitor closely to make sure that there was actually a problem or that he was truly ready to get up before I went in to check on him.

The waiting was difficult in the beginning, particularly if there was legitimate crying going on. I thankfully took my savvy mother's advice to look at the clock, because five minutes can feel like half an hour when you're listening to the wails of your most prized possession. Eventually giving Schnitzel some time to sort things out himself became my modus operandi and he, in turn, became an all-star self-soother. I am still amazed by some of the naps and nighttime snoozes he was able to "save" without help from my husband or me. He could wake up, cry for a solid five minutes, and then go back to sleep on his own like nothing had ever happened. All babies are different of course, but giving yours the time and space to learn how to calm herself can go a long way in helping her become less reliant on you.

Now for a brief word on independence generally, as it apparently means different things to different people. I know a mom who was always talking about how independent her baby was. She would frequently recount various "demands" that he had made, which she would then feel compelled to fulfill. He slept in her bed because he needed to nurse every couple of hours, and he wouldn't "allow" her to start weaning after a year because he was so independent. Say what?! This, my friends, is not independence. This is catering to your baby's every need and it is bound to make you go berserk sooner or later. You are the adult and you call the shots, even if they are going to temporarily upset your baby. Don't let him start thinking that he's in charge unless you are okay with him running your life for the next eighteen   years.

When In Doubt, Go Out

"There is life outside your apartment. I know it's hard to conceive. But there is life outside your apartment. And you're only going to see it if you leave."

~ Lyrics from one of the less memorable songs from the Tony award winning musical Avenue Q, but a useful reminder to first-time moms everywhere

I'd imagine that we all have at least one friend who had a baby and then promptly fell off the face of the earth. Some new parents seem to think that just because life has become decidedly more complicated, they need to hunker down for weeks, months, or even years. Personally, I wanted to avoid turning into a hermit at all costs when I had a baby. I was bound and determined to keep going out and doing things, even if it meant taking on the added stress and the extra ten pounds of gear to do them with my baby in tow. Frankly, I just figured I would be happier and feel more like myself during this major life transition if I regularly got out of the house and connected with the outside world.

Let's start with the baby steps, pun intended, of my going out approach. After my initial recovery period, I made it a point to leave my apartment at least once a day while I was on maternity leave. Sanity was the main goal here. Staying inside with your baby for long periods of time is bound to make you feel a bit nutty. Time just goes soooo slowwwly when you are confined to a handful of rooms for hours on end.

I came to truly appreciate this when the disastrous Camp Fire of 2018 blanketed Northern California with smoke and particulates, rendering a two-month-old Schnitzel and me housebound for a week. I was close to certifiably crazy by the time the smoke cleared. (As an aside, the more recent COVID-19 pandemic of 2020 has been way worse for the average mom in most respects, but thankfully has not warranted staying exclusively indoors due to dangerously toxic air quality. If anything, it has served as yet another reminder that we should all be getting our stroll on every day to preserve our collective sanity, baby or no baby.) But back to my maternity leave of 2018, I was pounding the pavement nearly every day it was safe to do so.

Strolling also became my default activity when I just didn't know what to do with Schnitzel. Oh, it's 4pm and he's fed, changed, wide awake, and I have no idea how I'm going to make it another two hours 'til Hubs gets home? Grab the carrier for the second or even third walk of the day! Getting some fresh air and a change of scenery almost always re-energized me, which is key when you're short on sleep and mental stimulation. This is not to say that I didn't spend a good amount of time on maternity leave binge-watching *Riverdale* (I did), but I also made a conscious effort to make sure that my butt wasn't starting to grow attached to the couch.

I realize the notion of getting out of the house on a daily basis may not seem earthshattering, but I mention it because I am continually surprised by how many new moms (or dads on paternity leave, for that matter) don't do it. On what I can only assume was our 832nd stroll together in the first three months of Schnitzel's life, I ran into a casual acquaintance and her baby at our neighborhood coffee shop. We had a nice chat and she remarked that it was her first time out of her apartment all week. *It was Friday.* No wonder she looked so shell-shocked. Additionally, I will admit that the Bay Area's mild climate made it easier for me to go out and about every day. If you happen to be on maternity leave in Minnesota in January (a fate that I actually willingly signed up for although it never came to fruition), my sincerest condolences. I would note, however, that Schnitzel spent a disproportionate amount of his first two years in Montana, so we're no strangers to cold weather outings. My solution was to get a cute AF snuggle suit and a JJ Cole Bundle Me and just get out there as much as possible. Baby sleds are also fun if you have access to snowy trails.

Beyond daily mileage, I am also a huge proponent of more ambitious outings with baby on a regular basis. It can be a complete hassle to get organized enough to get out the door, but it's refreshing to add some variety to an otherwise fairly monotonous existence. It's also liberating to do things that YOU actually want to do every once in a while. So what kinds of activities did Schnitzel and I do, you might ask? All sorts of things! Mom group (as you now know), mommy-and-me workout classes (multi-tasking at its finest), lunch dates and hikes with my friends (many of which involved an hour or two round trip in the car), and movies (a theater near us had "baby day" every Tuesday where the volume was lower and the employees more understanding). I aimed to do a couple of these field trips every week to keep things interesting.

Now, I have to be brutally honest. Some of these expeditions were epic fails or at least partial fails, especially in the early months. Don't even get me started on my sorry attempt at baby enrichment in the form of infant swim lessons. Schnitzel screamed the entire time while seemingly every other baby in our class splashed and squealed with glee. Unsurprisingly, I hung up the swim diaper after just three sessions. Then there is the dreaded public diaper blowout, which will almost certainly happen at the worst possible moment. But once you've handled the first poop-splosion out in the wild, it becomes much less intimidating. That is, as long as you haven't forgotten to pack a change of clothes — NEVER FORGET. While occasionally stressful, all of these escapades built up my confidence in handling my highly unpredictable small human and empowered me to continue living my life on mainly my own terms rather than being completely beholden to my baby.

Now for the next-level stuff — travel! Terrifying, I know. A lot of people will say it's just not worth it to travel with your baby. Personally, I think life is too short to stay home. Plus, traveling with your baby can be a really fun adventure if you have the right attitude. Some of my fondest memories of Schnitzel's early life were the various trips we did with him. By the time he turned one he had thirteen flights under his belt (half of which were cross country), his own MileagePlus account (for the one time we splurged on a seat for him – a red eye flight), and many non-memories of weekends away throughout Northern California. Instead of running through strategies for air travel, I'll just point you towards *Flying with Baby – The Essential Guide to Flying Domestically with Infants Under 1 Year Old*, a short eBook by Meg Collins, which will tell you everything you need to know. Car travel is more straightforward, thankfully, but accept that you'll likely need to make lots of stops and that your baby will invariably only pass out in the car seat precisely when you don't want her to and vice versa.

Again, not all of these trips were pretty. There were instances when we sat on the runway or in traffic for hours, which is exponentially more frustrating when you're dealing with a cranky baby who missed his nap. But I never regretted making the effort and my husband and I were stoked to realize that we could continue to travel much as we had in our pre-baby lives. These trips also had the positive side effect of bringing out the best in us as a dynamic parenting duo. It's one thing to handle your baby in the comfort of your own home. It's quite another to do so at 30,000 feet somewhere over Nebraska when he has a serious case of bad gas.

My last piece of advice on traveling is to do it regularly. By making travel a habit, you'll be more inclined to keep living your life on your own terms. You'll also be able to gradually adjust to the rapidly changing needs of your baby in a travel scenario. He will go from a snuggly worm who can be worn or packed around in an infant car seat to a wriggly, mobile critter who requires a constantly changing form of entertainment in a matter of months. Suffice it to say that you'll be much less intimidated to travel with the latter if you've been practicing and adapting during that transition.

Regardless of the stage, your high-level travel strategy should stay the same — plan meticulously, bring all the gear and snacks you think you might ever need, and expect that things will go wrong. But do yourself a favor and give it a go. There is life outside your apartment (and your city and state) and it can be pretty freaking awesome to share with your little one.

Embrace Babysitters

"I just wanted you to know that I feel like I'm channeling you today: I hired a sitter I've never met before and got the F out of the house so I could have some time to myself. I need to do this more often!!"

~ **Unsolicited text from a friend who had a toddler and a baby at the time**

I f you hadn't already guessed, I'm a big fan of babysitters. I think they should be a key component of any new mom's sanity plan.

However, I feel as if utilizing babysitters, particularly for an actual baby as opposed to older children, has become a bit passé. The mom martyrs would have us all believe that we need to spend every waking hour with our babies because no one else could possibly care for them as well. Calling on a babysitter is selfish and indulgent — what could you possibly need to do that is more important than spending time with your baby? And, if for some reason you absolutely have to go out alone, you best be feeling guilty about it. Your baby misses you.

Ladies, this is plain crazy talk. Do not let this narrative of guilt keep you from exercising the freedom you so desperately need as a new mom. Motherhood is the ultimate marathon and time for yourself needs to be a priority from the onset if you are going to thrive. For those of you lucky enough to have family members nearby, use them as much as you can. For the rest of us poor unfortunate souls who do not — babysitters all the way!

I first decided to leave Schnitzel with a babysitter when he was just under two months old, and to be fair, I wasn't really sure how I felt about it. I had my six-week check-up along with a postpartum glucose test for the prenatal diabetes I'm still not convinced I actually had, and the thought of toting Schnitzel along for the entire slate of activities was decidedly not appealing. Someone in my mom group had mentioned that her nanny's capable daughter was available for babysitting most mornings, so I got her number and texted her on a whim the night before my appointment. When she responded that she'd be there at 9am, I felt both excited and nervous.

The next day I couldn't have been more pleased with the decision. I actually got to have an undistracted conversation with my OBGYN about my recovery, and I wasn't worried about trying to attend to Schnitzel without exerting myself too much so as to botch the glucose test. (One simply should not have to drink that viscous Kool-Aid crap any more times than is absolutely necessary). And when I came home, I found Schnitzel getting along splendidly with the babysitter. I was also unreasonably excited to see him again even though I'd only been gone for a few hours. Turns out absence really does make the heart grow fonder.

I was so pleased with this initial foray into ad hoc childcare that I asked this same babysitter to come for a few hours one morning a week for the rest of my maternity leave. Some weeks I would go to appointments for postpartum related treatment or run errands that would have otherwise been difficult to get done. But just as often I would do something completely decadent like go for a run or swim, get a mani/pedi, or grab the latest *US Weekly* and take myself out for a leisurely breakfast. I refused to feel bad about these outings since I knew Schnitzel was in good hands, and I relished the autonomy and time to myself. Moreover, the workouts and the pampering had an important "look good, feel good" effect on my somewhat fragile postpartum psyche. I would look forward to my me-time every week, especially if my husband happened to be traveling for work, as then it was legitimately the only time I had for myself. And I always came back home to Schnitzel feeling more relaxed, happy, and excited to see him. It was good for both of us.

While the weekday morning babysitter was our steady Eddy, she had limited availability and I soon found it necessary to branch out to other babysitters when something came up or I simply wanted to plan a date night. (Don't let date nights fall off your or your partner's radar now that you are parents — they are important!) I was always a little nervous leaving him with someone new, but I never once regretted it. In a true show of faith in babysitters, I left a then ten-week-old Schnitzel with a babysitter at our hotel in Sonoma for a solid eight hours while my husband and I attended a good friend's wedding. And you know what? Everything was just fine, except for my hangover the next day.

I am always taken aback when I meet other moms with babies, or in some case full blown toddlers, who say they have never left their child alone with someone other than a family member. My first thought is usually, "Good grief, girl, get a life!" But even beyond that, I personally think it's a great idea for a baby to get used to being around someone other than his parents. Eventually you'll have to go back to work or something will prevent you or your partner from being able to be around, and there is less likelihood for serious drama if this isn't y'all's first rodeo. One friend of mine who had serious anxiety about letting others watch her first child underscored this notion in admitting that it would've been a lot better to start with babysitters earlier so it wasn't such a big mental hurdle.

The pushback I sometimes hear from these babysitter-resistant folks is that they just can't find anyone they trust. I mean, I sort of understand that sentiment. It is your baby after all. But I would venture to say you can probably overcome this if you put in a little effort. Ask all your local mom friends if they have recommendations, and if that doesn't generate leads get on UrbanSitter or Care.com and skim profiles and reviews. These platforms also allow you to correspond with babysitters, and you may even be able to conduct a short interview with some prior to booking. It can certainly be a little intimidating to hire someone you haven't met in person, but if you're overly concerned, arrange to have them come over early so you can spend an hour getting ready or doing chores before you leave while surreptitiously keeping an eye on how they are interacting with your baby.

I recommend dipping your toe in the babysitting pool early on so both you and your baby get used to the idea, and aiming to build a bench of babysitters who are available at different times so you won't be scrambling when you really need someone. Additionally, don't fret if you find that your babysitter didn't do everything exactly the way you would have. Everyone has their own way of doing things and children are quite adaptable. As long as your child is safe, well attended to, and treated with kindness and compassion, it really doesn't matter if the babysitter used the wrong ointment or gave your baby too much milk.

Lastly, with babysitters in your arsenal, there's no reason why being a mom means you have to bid your social life adieu. When an invite pops up, try to make your default answer "yes" instead of "no." There's a good chance that if you commit to something first, you'll inevitably find a childcare solution in the interim. If there are friends you haven't caught up with lately or events you really want to attend, take the initiative to make it happen. More than anything, never beat yourself up or let anyone else make you feel bad for going out and doing something you want to do. Taking care of a tiny human is intense, and you've definitely earned as many breaks as you want.

Childcare Is A Moving Target

"Things change. And friends leave. Life doesn't stop for anybody."

~ Stephen Chbosky, author of
The Perks of Being a Wallflower

Not long before Schnitzel's first birthday, we decided to escape the cold, foggy summer in San Francisco to visit some friends in Southern California. It was his first beach day ever and it was glorious. I was basking in the sun while he was endlessly entertained by the sand and the scene. Then I noticed a text from the mom that we had been doing a nanny share[6] with for the past seven months asking if I had a minute to chat. My stomach dropped. This vague type of question is almost never good. I tried to un-see it, but then realized my worries would eat me alive if I didn't just rip off the Band-Aid and call her immediately.

With the waves crashing in the background, the other mom went through a short preamble about how doing nanny share together had been really fantastic and all, but her son had unexpectedly gotten off a

---

[6] A nanny share is when two families with children around the same age team up and have a single nanny watch both children at the same time while splitting the cost.

waitlist for a preschool and they were going to send him there next month. Gut punch. We had been enjoying what was quite possibly the world's most convenient nanny share - she lived in the other unit in my building which saved us from time consuming drop-offs and schlepping gear around — and we had planned to continue this arrangement at least through the end of the year. I didn't have anything constructive to say to her, so I asked a couple of polite questions about the preschool and quickly hung up. I had less than one month to find a new childcare solution and the clock was ticking. My perfect beach weekend suddenly had an ominous black cloud hanging over it.

The next two months were sheer frustration and I swear to God my gray hairs multiplied to reflect my angst. I wanted to stay with our nanny and vice versa, but despite posting on seemingly every childcare-related and local mom forum I could find, I had a terrible time finding interested families. It may have been a slow time of year, an awkward age for Schnitzel to find a good match, or just flat out bad luck, who knows. One mom that we did reciprocal house visits/playdates with straight up ghosted me when I tried to follow up. WTF, was this as bad as dating?! To make matters worse, Schnitzel was also very lonely without a pal during this period and was unusually clingy every morning when I tried to leave for work. Thankfully, another wonderful family decided to join us after nearly a month of courting and after we had paid a small fortune (i.e. our nanny's one child rate) during the interim period. I was relieved but exhausted.

In hindsight, I could have made this whole thing easier on myself had I maintained a more flexible and optimistic mindset. I thought my original nanny share was the be-all-end-all and I had expected it to last forever, or at least for the informally agreed upon year. Beyond that, I really felt wronged by the other family's decision to move on, and quite frankly I had a negative attitude towards finding a new family.

While far from an ideal scenario, I came to realize that nothing about my situation was unique. Nanny shares are wonderful from a money saving and child socialization standpoint, but they fall apart all the time due to the increased complexity in logistics and interpersonal dynamics that come with having three distinct parties. The mom in my original nanny share was well within her rights to send her child to preschool per the terms we had agreed upon in the contract between our families. And when it comes downs to it, I truly believe that every parent is just trying to make the best decision for their child and themselves.

While nanny shares may be especially vulnerable to change, other childcare options may not have the longevity you would hope for either. People move. Teachers turnover. Schedules change. Personalities and philosophies clash. Logistics become too cumbersome. Or if it's 2020, COVID-19 happens and hardly anyone has childcare for a while. In short, childcare is tricky and all too often life gets in the way. Just because you are happy or unhappy with your current situation doesn't mean that will always be the case. Should you find yourself searching for a new childcare arrangement, try to keep an open mind and you may be pleasantly surprised with the results. I'm happy to report that our second nanny share family, while less geographically desirable, turned out to be a better fit as their son was closer in age to Schnitzel than the original family's boy. Some things happen for a reason.

A good friend had warned me that childcare was a moving target, but I didn't truly appreciate it until I experienced my first hiccup. If you go in expecting that there will be unforeseen challenges along the way, you'll be in a much better position to take the changes in stride and get on with your life.

Fake It 'Til You Make It

"I didn't fully wrap my head around the fact that there would be a person at the end of it. I read endlessly about pregnancy and what to eat and what not to eat. And then I sort of prepared not at all for the actual baby."

~ Ellie Kemper, actress and comedian

As you've no doubt realized, I had a lot of strong opinions regarding how I wanted my motherhood experience to be. One area I was keenly focused on was my overall outlook on navigating the incredible new challenge of caring for a child, as well as the image I portrayed to both myself and the world. Simply put, I vehemently rejected the exasperated mom archetype that so frequently turns up in everyday life. Turning into the tired, harried mom who has a nest on top of her head, has been wearing the same yoga pants for five days straight, and is sent into a tailspin over seemingly every tiny thing her child does was my worst nightmare. Yet when I became a mom, I was surprised to see how many moms played into this paradigm. Follow a handful of popular mom-oriented Instagram accounts and you'll see a great deal of "my life's a mess, my kid's a jerk, woe is me, time for wine" posts. I know they are partly in jest and I understand why the sentiment resonates because, let's be honest, all moms feel that way sometimes. However, I just can't get behind playing the victim on the regular.

This is not to say that I aspired to be the annoyingly put together mom either. I was never going to be the mom who knows all of the latest on tongue ties and baby-led weaning and Montessori beds, who only leaves the house with a fabulous outfit and full face of makeup, and who loves to tell everyone how great things are and how everything about being a mom is magical. Nope. When I started down the path to motherhood, I just aimed to be the mom who was pretty happy, relatively sane, and mostly had things under control. How hard could that be?

Well, I discovered pretty quickly that it's challenging to attain even that middle ground, at least in the beginning. The learning curve was steep and despite having read a few books and taken a couple of classes, everything seemed completely foreign to me in real life. It's also borderline impossible to feel in control if you aren't entirely comfortable with your new role. Imposter syndrome -- when you feel that you're in a position you really shouldn't be in -- can be very real. There were many times in those early days when I would look at Schnitzel and think "that can't possibly be my baby," as my hands turned clammy. My mom also took to occasionally referring to me "Little Mama," which really threw me for a loop. *Me? A mama? Whoa, whoa, whoa.* And because I didn't have a lot of confidence in my baby care abilities, I spent an inordinate amount of time thinking through complex decisions trees of what my next move with Schnitzel should be. I was really all up in my head.

However, upon talking to other moms I realized that all of these feelings were totally normal. No first-time mom really has it all figured out even if it might appear that way. We are all pretty much experimenting and learning on the fly. And while there may be some women who immediately feel like natural moms, it's a more gradual process for many. I felt so much better when a friend with a two-year-old told me she was still occasionally weirded out when she thought too much about said two-year-old belonging to her. Moreover, I learned that the totally mundane baby care decisions I would re-think one hundred times over really didn't matter. A baby's needs are pretty darn simple in the beginning and no one decision is likely to make or break them (or you).

While I certainly took comfort in knowing that I wasn't any more clueless or paranoid than the next first-time mom out there, I still didn't love feeling like an amateur. As such, I figured I might as well try to flip the script on my entire new mom psyche. I had gone through several presentation trainings in my professional life and learned that you could trick yourself into feeling more confident through tactics such as power posing and positive self-talk. Mind over matter, in a nutshell. Leveraging this concept, I thought that perhaps if I could stay calm and pretend to be the self-assured, in-control mom I aspired to be, maybe (just maybe!) I would actually turn into that mom.

My first big test came when Schnitzel was two months old and I decided to fly to Montana with him — alone. I was still on maternity leave and figured going up to visit my parents would be a pleasant break from the city. Beyond that, I was eager to get back to traveling. To say I was wound up about the trip would be an understatement. I packed and re-packed for close to a week prior to the trip and had unsettling dreams the night before. But when my alarm went off the next morning, it was game on. I showered, put on a respectable outfit, and did my hair and makeup since looking put together was part of convincing myself that I was, in fact, put together. Then I got Schnitzel fed and ready to go and we headed off to the airport.

From that moment on I exuded confidence as I knocked out the requisite pre-flight tasks, despite being terrified of the infinite number of mishaps that could have occurred. Check bags and obtain infant boarding pass. Boom. Strap baby in carrier for security and fold up stroller. Boom. Last minute nurse and diaper change before flight. Boom. Ask to use an open seat on the plane and carry Schnitzel on in his car seat. Nailed it. I had to contend with some in-flight squirminess and awkward public nursing, but overall the trip went off without a major hitch and I felt as if I had conquered the world. I even garnered some positive attention and kudos from fellow passengers for my performance. This was not an image of the exasperated mom losing her mind over the stress of flying alone with her baby for the first time. This was the image of a mom who had simply acted like she was a seasoned pro. I had faked my way to victory!

One of the great things about the fake it 'til you make it approach is that it reinforces itself. The more you pretend like you're competent, the more likely it is that you'll actually feel like you are. And each small success, such as my solo flight experience, builds all-important confidence. Moreover, your baby will likely pick up on your vibe too. I'm told that babies can sense emotions, and I don't believe it's a coincidence that the distraught moms seem to have the cranky kids while the relaxed, confident moms seem to have the happy-go-lucky ones. There's a feedback loop there, and while it can certainly go both ways, you alone have control over your own mindset and actions. Don't waste that opportunity.

Regularly utilizing this mental hack helped me grow into the kind of mom I hoped to be…at least most days. There will undoubtedly be times when things go awry and you react poorly regardless of what your overarching attitude is. But don't set yourself up to fail before you've even begun. Lastly, for the love of all things holy, reject the notion of that your life is going to be a mess simply because you have a child. It doesn't need to become a self-fulfilling prophecy.

While I do love the premise of fake it 'til you make it, I do feel compelled to admit that I don't think any mom ever truly "makes it." I eventually grew more at ease with my role as a mom and legitimately more confident in my abilities. But I also discovered that just when I felt I had the ins and outs of one childhood stage mastered, it was likely on its way out. It seems to me that being a mom is a continuous learning process and the best things you can do are get comfortable with the uncomfortable, stay optimistic, maintain your sense of humor, and enjoy the ride.

Mom Is Only Part Of Your Identity

"Remember the woman you were before you had kids. She's still in there. Take care of her."

~ One of the better popular mom quotes floating around the internet

One of the reasons I put off having a baby for so long was I really liked my life the way it was. I had a solid career, a rich social life, and I got to indulge in all sorts of other passions from traveling to running marathons to volunteering. Simply put, I found being me pretty fulfilling. I knew that having a baby was going be a profound change, but I didn't know exactly in which ways. I had heard about mothers "losing themselves," and I desperately wanted to ensure that being a mom wasn't going to completely consume me.

As you may have guessed from my earlier discussion on imposter syndrome, I got off to a strong start in retaining my individual identity. In spite of taking care of Schnitzel around the clock during the first couple weeks of his life, I was still all about me. When I took him to the pediatrician for the first time and the receptionist asked "Patient's Name?" I replied "Emily" without hesitation. "Your son's name is Emily?" she remarked, unimpressed. Clearly, I hadn't yet adapted to my new mom status. I managed to repeat this mistake in subsequent visits over the next few weeks as it took me some time to realize that I was no longer the sole center of my universe.

Then, seemingly out of nowhere, the switch flipped. It was all about Schnitzel, all the time. I spammed my friends with his pictures. I paraded him around San Francisco and willed strangers to ogle him and gush over his chubby cheeks. I started nearly every conversation with something Schnitzel-related. I changed my online passwords to have a Schnitzel reference. You get the picture. On the one hand, this was a good thing. I was getting accustomed to my new role as a mom and was eager to share my enthusiasm for my baby with the world. On the other hand, I was starting to get so wrapped up in the whirlwind of my mommyhood that I was beginning to forget about the other things made me "me."

An impromptu self-intervention came several weeks later with the delivery of my Peloton, a truly amazing, if expensive, workout option for busy moms. When I was prompted to enter a username I immediately typed in *SchnitzelsMom*. Then I paused. Was a piece of breaded meat's mother what I really wanted to portray to the world? While somewhat of a trivial question given that this an online community comprised mainly of people I'd never met, it did make me stop and think. Did I want everyone to know I was a mom? Indubitably. I was and continue to be extremely proud of that. But in that moment, I realized that I was starting to become a tad one dimensional. I made a strong course correction and typed in my slightly provocative AOL screenname from college. Yep. And let me just say that if I have offended anyone who has already dubbed themselves "so and so's mom" in a public forum, please know that I actually think that's great. For me personally, it just happened to serve as the point of recognition that the melding of my identity with my child's had gone too far.

Loss of identity for moms is completely understandable given how wonderful, demanding, and generally all-consuming young children can be. But it also seems like a difficult and lonely way to live life. Thankfully my brush with identity loss was early (during maternity leave), shallow, and brief. To restore my balance after the Peloton incident, I tried to think of my mom status as an integral part of my now arguably richer and more complex identity, rather than my defining characteristic. I also began to use the odd periods of downtime that maternity leave affords to reconnect with old acquaintances and check in with faraway friends — and not just those with kids. Not only did these exchanges bring me joy and make me feel less isolated, but they also gave me a way to share my exciting life updates while simultaneously reminding myself that I was still largely the same person I was before I became a mom.

While on maternity leave, I also tried to stay grounded by finding small ways to be productive that had nothing to do with my baby. I learned early on that as a new mom you need to let go of your long to-do list. It's a losing game. By the time you've crossed off one item, you'll have added three more. The trick is to find fulfilling mini-projects that can be spread across the odd ten-minute segments over a series of days and weeks or even months. My crowning achievements during leave were ordering furniture for my dining room, coaching two clients on their business school applications, and re-attaining very limited proficiency in German via a daily session on Duolingo (I felt I owed it to Schnitzel not to be a complete poser). A more industrious friend of mine started a children's teepee business on Amazon from her living room on her first maternity leave and repainted her entire apartment on her second. Whatever your ambition level, tangible accomplishments such as these can go a long way in making you feel like your life is not singularly dedicated to baby care.

I also tried to make sure that I did something every day that was just for me. Occasionally it was something big like meeting up with a friend, but more often it was something small such as a short workout or a glass of wine and some online shopping before bed. These small indulgences are crucial for new moms everywhere and should be prioritized even if they come at the expense of tidying up the kitchen, organizing toys, or washing poopy onesies. Make your partner wash the poopy onesies if at all possible.

When my maternity leave ended and I returned to work however, I found myself face-to-face with the identity challenge once again. First of all, I had enjoyed my leave and I found it difficult to leave Schnitzel at home and get back to the grind. I would spend hours sitting at my desk scrolling through photos of him on my phone and eagerly awaiting our nanny's next update. Between that and pumping every three hours in a glorified closet, it's a wonder I got anything done in my first month back. But as melancholy as I felt during the transition back to work, I ultimately decided that my career was an important part of who I was and that I wanted to continue building it even it sucked for a while.

Secondly, even though my life had fundamentally changed, I didn't want to portray that to the majority of my co-workers. Although I wanted to show them pictures of my darling Schnitzel and gratuitously insert stories about him into casual conversation, I tried my hardest to show restraint. I didn't want to be the mom who is always talking about her kid, which I remembered can be really uncomfortable for people who have zero interest in kids. Once again, I had to consciously decide that "working mom" was a part of my narrative, but not my entire narrative. I struck a balance in sharing all the Schnitzel details with the co-workers I was closest with or that routinely demonstrated an interest, but otherwise keeping them to myself unless prompted.

And while I'm on the topic of going back to work, I would highly recommend the book *Back to Work After Baby: How to Plan and Navigate a Mindful Return from Maternity Leave* by Lori Mihalich-Levin for helpful guidance and support regarding all aspects of this tricky and emotional transition. Lori also leads a Mindful Return eCourse (mindfulreturn.com) several times a year which builds on many of the ideas in this book — self-care, confidence, and community, among others — and provides a forum for connecting with other moms who are going through the same experience.

While working moms certainly face a daunting set of challenges, it may be even a taller task for stay at home moms (SAHM) to maintain a strong sense of self as they cannot rely on a job to provide structure and a de facto purpose outside of being a mom. While I can't directly speak to this particular challenge, my advice to SAHMs would be to identify and make time for fulfilling endeavors outside of childcare, even if it means hiring some part-time help. Whether it's freelancing, volunteering, writing, or training to become a pilates instructor, you just gotta have something else going on besides your baby. And it's perhaps even more important for SAHMs to also make time for self-care and time with friends, given how physically and mentally exhausting being a full-time caretaker can be. I have many happy and fulfilled SAHM friends in my life and what they all have in common is they have found productive outlets for their talents outside of their kids while making sure they also have adequate support and some time for themselves.

Regardless of how you choose to spend your days, do not under any circumstances let becoming a mother negatively affect your self-worth. I came across a post on a popular mom-focused Instagram account that said in big block letters, *"I'm nowhere near the woman I was before kids and I'm cool with that."* What the actual fuck. Even if taken as joke, what kind of message does that send to the 100,000 moms who follow this dimwit? Whether you're in the office all day, at home, or somewhere in between, you are undoubtedly hustling your butt off every day. More than that, you are the center of one person's entire world and there's no greater impact than that. Sure, it may feel like you are juggling too many things and not able to devote your full effort to any one area, but that's just part of life sometimes. Being a mom is the hardest and most important job in the world and you should feel damn proud for living it each and every day.

And now that I've highlighted one specific piece of garbage on social media, let me take this opportunity to be a real Debbie Downer and encourage you to limit your social media intake all together. I know, I know, social media seems like a lifeline when you are alone all day with a non-conversant love mound and in need of some mindless adult content. I'll even admit that social media does have some virtues — remember my earlier praise of Facebook mom groups? That being said, too much social media can be extremely detrimental to your new mom psyche, particularly if you are doubting your abilities or trying to come to terms with your new and different life, body, or identity.

As one of my mom friends quipped "I personally find Instagram to be rather toxic as it just multiples whatever your biggest insecurities are." Another friend noted that she routinely found herself in a pit of self-loathing as she struggled to fit into her pre-baby wardrobe while being served up a constant visual stream of celebrities, friends, and randos in advertisements who seemingly had no problem losing their baby weight. And these certainly aren't isolated experiences. Research has shown that we frequently underestimate the degree to which others are putting on a positive show on social media, a misperception which can make us feel inadequate, and that spending time on social media can increase loneliness and decrease satisfaction with life. So, if you're starting to feel like every other mom out there has a cuter baby or a more glamorous life, perhaps do yourself a favor and quit checking your phone every five minutes. I bet that nine times out of ten you'll feel better having spent that time admiring your precious nugget and appreciating what a badass you are instead.

This is one of the longest chapters in this book and that is intentional. I truly feel that preserving your sense of self is one of the biggest keys to thriving as a mom. Kids demand so much of what we have to offer — time, energy, love, money (ha!) — that it's easy for them to quickly become *the* focal point of our lives. But I'm convinced that a life dedicated to serving someone else isn't optimal. In fact, it seems like a fast track to burnout. I've found great satisfaction in continuing to honor my pre-motherhood values and desires, while celebrating the new dimension that being a mom has given me.

Parting Shots

"Just like you did not know what an orgasm was before you had one, nature does not let you know how great children are until you have them. Children are the orgasm of life."

~ The Original Lululemon Manifesto

(Yes, this actually used to be printed on their shopping bags in 2003, in case you needed any more motivation to buy stretchy pants).

I felt a flood of conflicting emotions the day Schnitzel turned one, much like I had in the delivery room exactly a year earlier. I was happy that my baby was healthy and full of life (and that he wore his cute suspenders and birthday crown all day). I was grateful to be celebrating with both sets of grandparents, who had all flown in for the occasion, and a wonderful group of close friends and their kids. I was sad that he wasn't technically a baby anymore and worried that I was already beginning to forget some of the magical memories of the first year. And I was perplexed that I could feel so happy and sad at the same time. Perhaps more than anything, I felt proud.

Many friends congratulated me on having survived the first year, and although that seemed over-the-top to me initially, I soon came to agree with the sentiment. Having a baby is not for the faint of heart. A baby requires an inordinate amount of time, effort, patience, and courage. Every. Single. Day. There is no off switch, for your baby or your overwhelmed brain. And there is quite possibly nothing that can prepare a first-time mom for this sort of prolonged intensity. You just have to take a deep breath and take it one day at a time.

While proud of keeping my favorite tiny human alive during his most vulnerable days, my biggest triumph was undoubtedly my personal growth during this time. First of all, my attitude towards children had done a complete 180. I had gone from someone who thought babies ruined everything to a veritable baby champion. This meant I had a lot more empathy for my friends with kids and for fellow moms everywhere. I was kinder and more understanding. I also appreciated my parents even more. Looking back, I was a bit embarrassed by how negative I had been about having kids. I just didn't get it. But then again, it's near impossible to fully grasp until you're in the middle of it.

Secondly, becoming a mom had helped me grow in ways that surprised and delighted me. My executive function had increased tenfold as I got lots of practice adapting on the fly and trouble-shooting all sorts of predicaments. I got much better at asking for help and advice — something that's always been hard for me. I learned to make meaningful sacrifices — another thing that's always been hard for me. I became a lot more comfortable with uncertainty. I started cutting myself some slack when I didn't live up to my high standards. And in spite of the increased complexity of life and additional responsibilities, I learned to be more present. I simply wanted to soak up every minute I had with those who mattered the most to me.

I was also proud that I had managed to stay true to myself throughout this year of extraordinary change. In many ways, I was still very much the same person I had been pre-baby. I continued to take joy and satisfaction in my marriage, my friendships, my work, and my interests. I could easily have conversations with people who had no interest in kids. I did not become singularly defined by being a mother. Against all odds, the personal transformation that had occurred had been nothing but additive to the "old me" that I had been so worried about losing in motherhood.

In hindsight, I believe that taking ownership of my experience as a new mom was key to making my transition to motherhood smoother than I ever could've imagined. I had a clear idea of what I wanted motherhood to look like, and I took deliberate steps to try to make my vision a reality. I prioritized my mental and physical health. I took breaks and did things for myself and refused to feel bad about it. I convinced myself that I was a capable, put-together mom who had things under control instead of giving into the chaos that motherhood can entail. And I didn't buy in to the hoopla that comes with having a baby or feel the need to breastfeed for a year, co-sleep, or go to baby music class three times a week simply because that's what society seemingly expected from me. Nay. I made my own decisions based on what worked best for me and my baby.

It is my hope that you will be able to take some of my principles and apply to them to your own journey as a first-time mom as you see fit. Whatever you do, please be kind to yourself and don't let anyone tell you what you should or shouldn't be doing when it comes to your baby. This incredible experience is yours, and yours only. And you're going to nail it. You got this, mama.

About The Author

E mily Lammers is a financial services professional, admissions consultant, career coach, marketer, writer, and mom of two. She enjoys opining on a variety of topics in written form, and tries to inject her commentary with authenticity and humor whenever possible. Across all of her pursuits, she has a strong desire to communicate useful ideas and help empower people to reach their potential and lead fulfilling lives. Emily specifically tackles career, money, and mom life on her blog www.emilyexplainsitall.com.

Emily found that becoming a mother, while certainly challenging, didn't need to be the anxiety-filled, life-altering event that it had so frequently been made out to be. She was inspired to share her experience in order to provide support, encouragement, and helpful advice to other new moms.

Emily is a proud Montana native and obtained an undergraduate degree from Princeton University and an MBA from the Haas School of Business, University of California – Berkeley.

Made in the USA
Columbia, SC
18 May 2022